Seasonal for Busy Hands

Fine-Motor Skills for Little Learners

Build skills year round!

- Cutting
- Coloring
- Tracing
- Drawing
- Tearing
- Crumpling

Managing Editor: Kimberly Brugger-Murphy

Editorial Team: Becky S. Andrews, Diane Badden, Kimberley Bruck, Karen A. Brudnak, Kitty Campbell, Pam Crane, Lynette Dickerson, Sarah Foreman, Tazmen Hansen, Marsha Heim, Lori Z. Henry, Debra Liverman, Dorothy C. McKinney, Thad H. McLaurin, Brenda Miner, Sharon Murphy, Jennifer Nunn, Mark Rainey, Greg D. Rieves, Hope Rodgers, Donna K. Teal

93 Seasonal Practice Pages!

www.themailbox.com

ISBN10 #1-56234-832-9 • ISBN13 #978-156234-832-8

Manufactured in the United States
10 9 8 7 6 5 4 3 2 1

Table of Contents

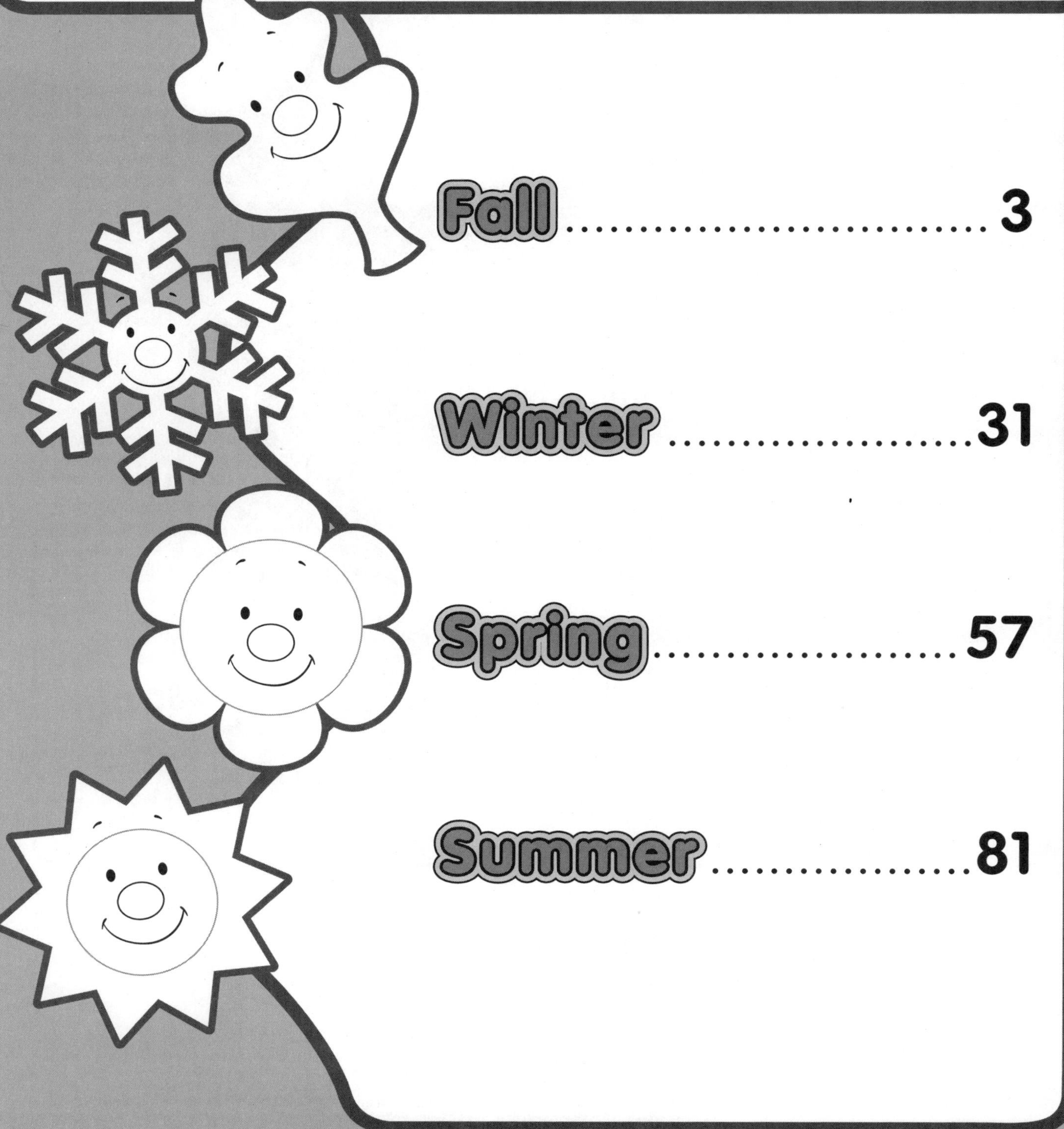

Name

Back in the Box

Trace.

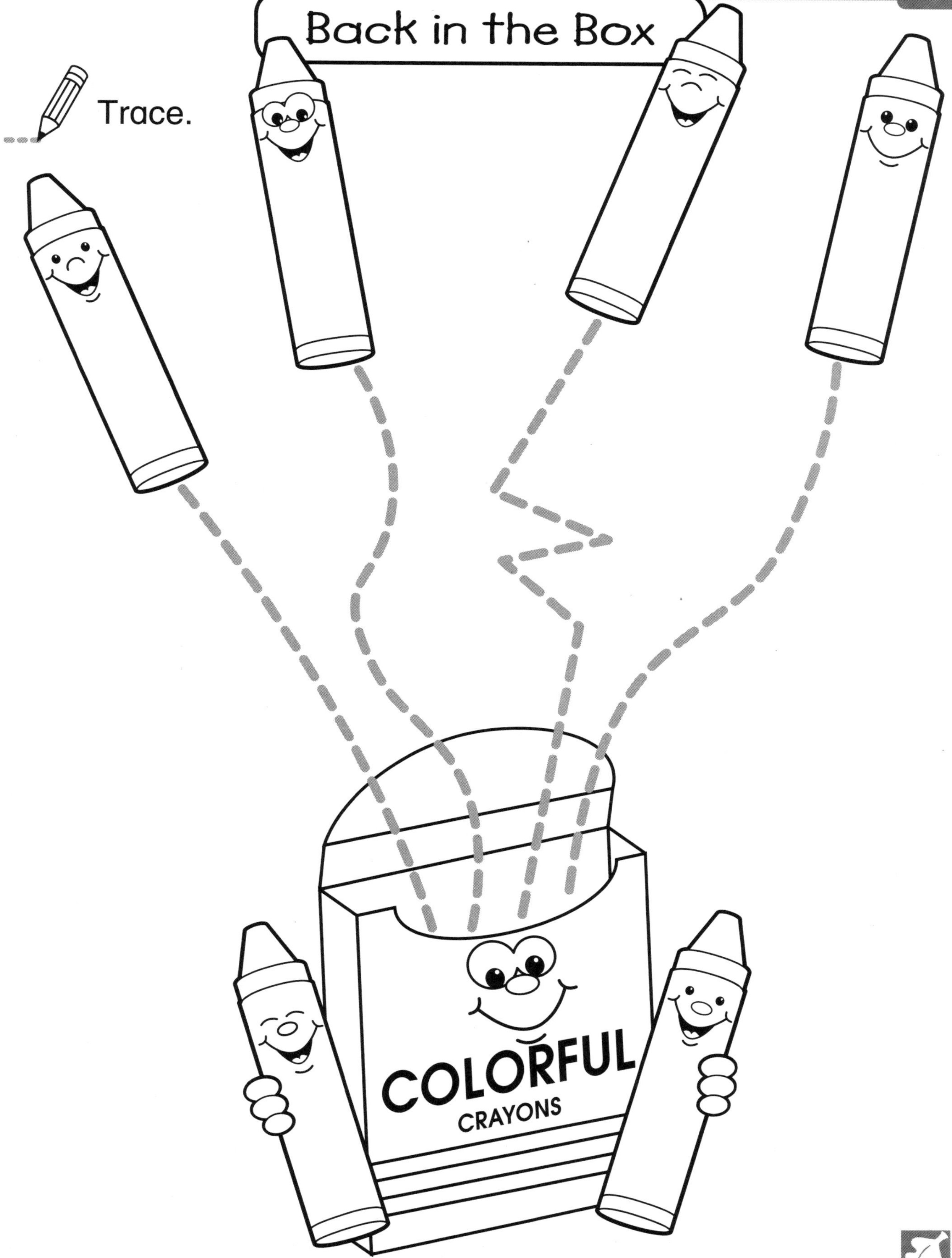

Name

Scooping Seeds!

Tear.

Glue.

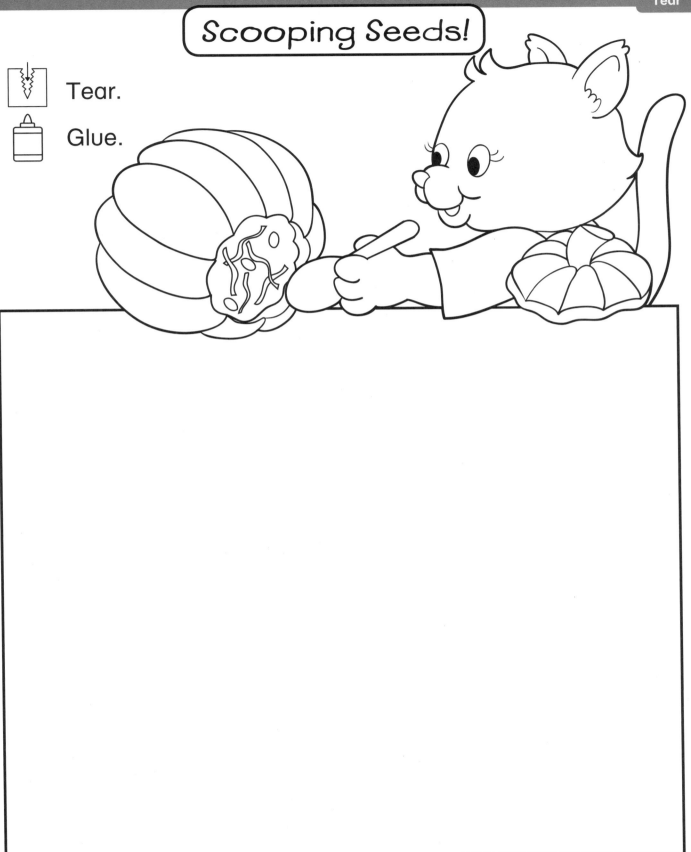

Note to the teacher: Have students tear white and orange construction paper and glue it to the box so it resembles pumpkin seeds and pulp.

Name

Barn Bats

Trace.

Name

Pumpkin-Picking Time!

Trace.

Crumple.

Glue.

Note to the teacher: Have students crumple squares of orange tissue paper and glue them to the pumpkin.

Name

Trick-or-Treat Trail

Trace.

Name

A Treat to Eat!

Color.

Name

Friendly Scarecrow

Cut.

Name

Midnight Snack

Crumple.

Glue.

Note to the teacher: Have students crumple squares of yellow, purple, and orange tissue paper and then glue them to the corn so it resembles an ear of Indian corn.

Name

Crows and Crops

Cut.

Glue.

Name

Cut.

Glue.

Hooray for Hayrides!

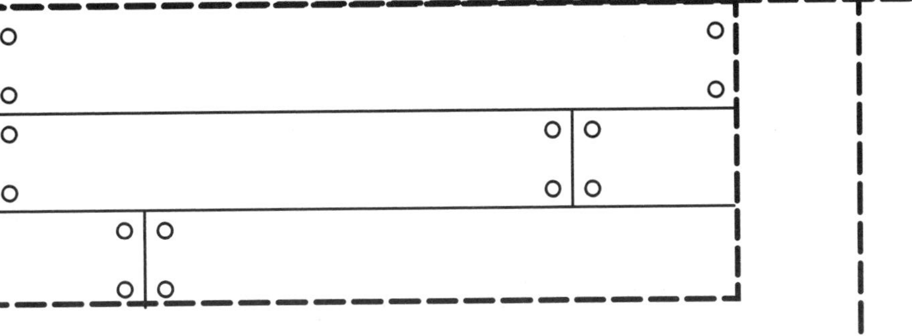

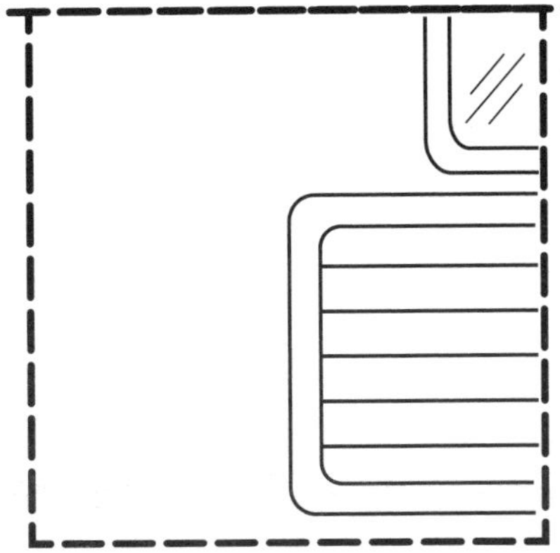

Name

Horn of Plenty

Color.

Name

Sailing to America

Trace.

Mayflower

Name

Fancy Feathers

 Tear.

 Glue.

Note to the teacher: Have students tear paper and glue it to the turkeys so it resembles tail feathers.

Name

Cut

Thanksgiving Feast

Cut.

Name

Peas, Please!

Crumple.

Glue.

Note to the teacher: Have students crumple squares of green tissue paper and glue them to the plate so they resemble peas.

Name

Smells So Good!

Trace.

Name

Bread and Butter

Cut.

Name

Whirling and Twirling!

Trace.

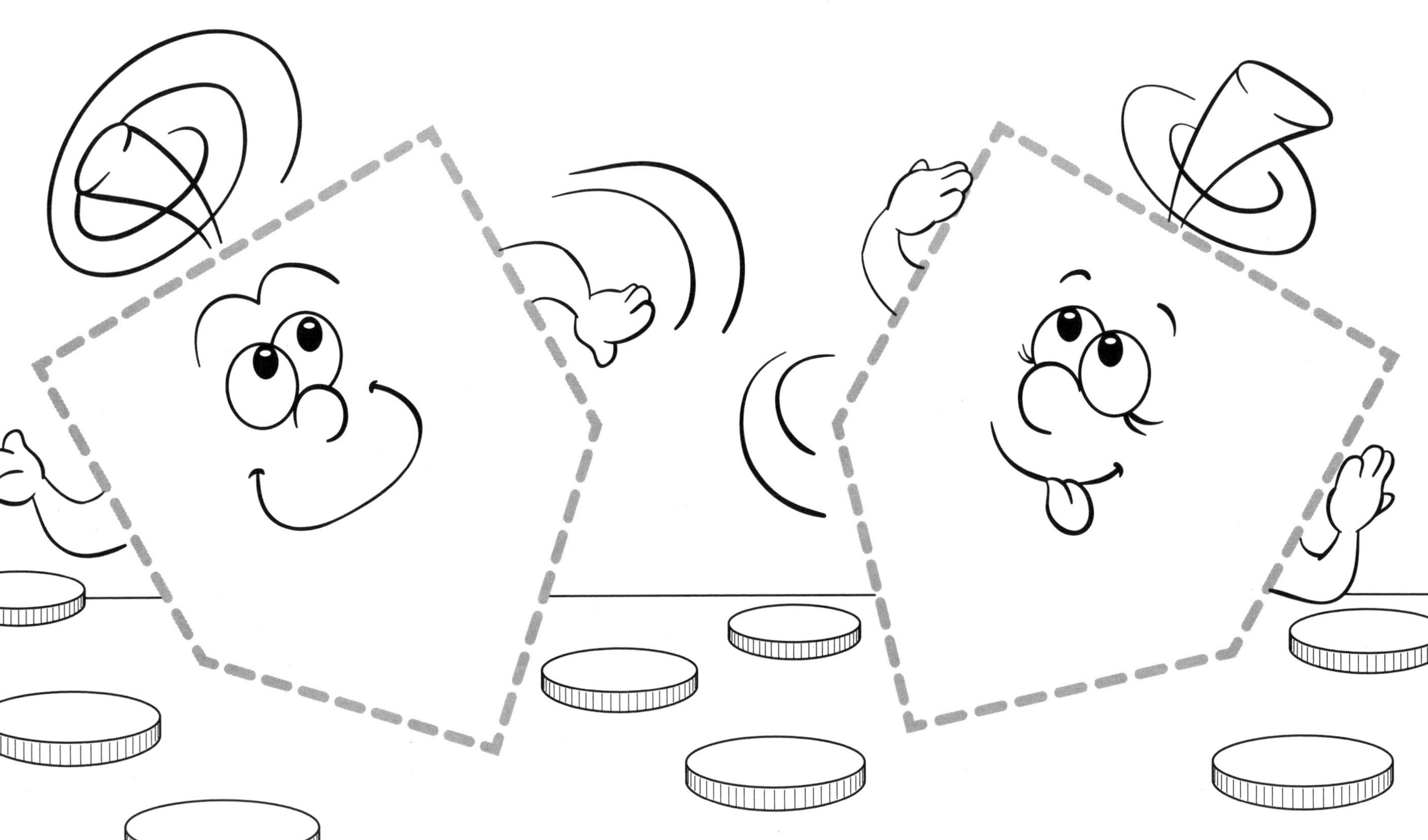

Name

Light Up the Night

Crumple.

Glue.

Note to the teacher: Have students crumple pieces of yellow tissue paper and glue them above the candles so they resemble flames.

Name

Colorful Candy Cane

Color.

Name

Kitty's Lights

Trace.

Name

Santa's Hats

Trace.

Crumple.

Glue.

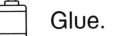

Note to the teacher: After the child finishes tracing, have him crumple five squares of white tissue paper and glue each one to the top of a different hat.

Cozy Stockings

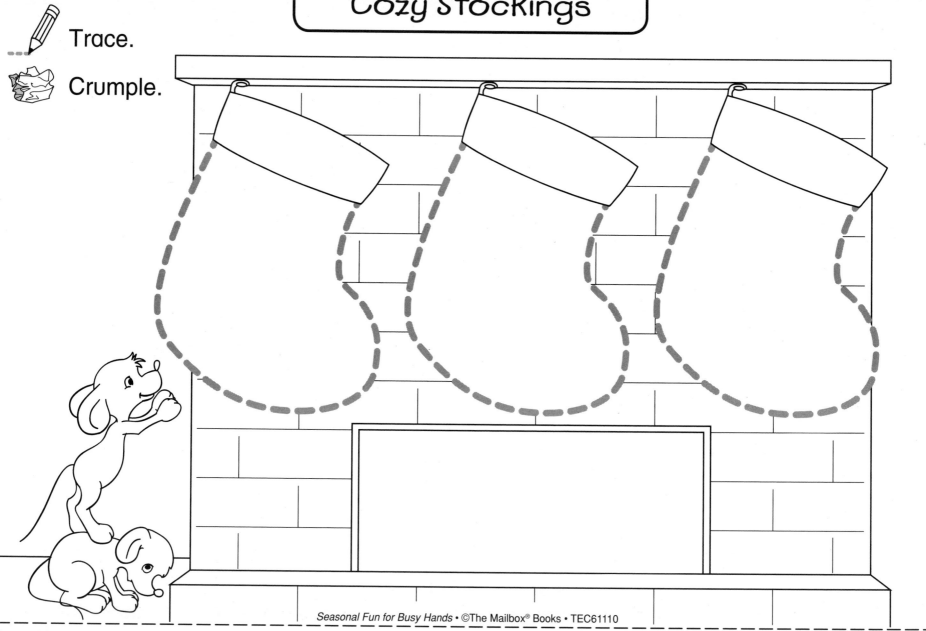

Trace.

Crumple.

Note to the teacher: After the child finishes tracing, have her crumple orange tissue paper squares and glue them to the fireplace so they resemble flames.

Name

Go, Rudolph!

Tear.

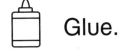

Crumple.

Glue.

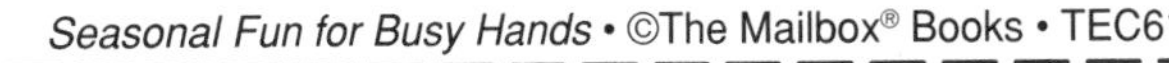

Note to the teacher: Have students tear white facial tissue and then glue the pieces around Rudolph so they resemble snow. Then have each child crumple a small piece of red tissue paper and glue it to Rudolph's nose.

Name

Sweet Fellow

Finish the gingerbread man.

Note to the teacher: If desired, copy the page onto brown paper. After students have finished their drawings, have them drizzle white paint on their gingerbread men so it resembles frosting.

Name

Pretty Presents

Cut.

Glue.

Name

Cut.

My Mkeka

Name

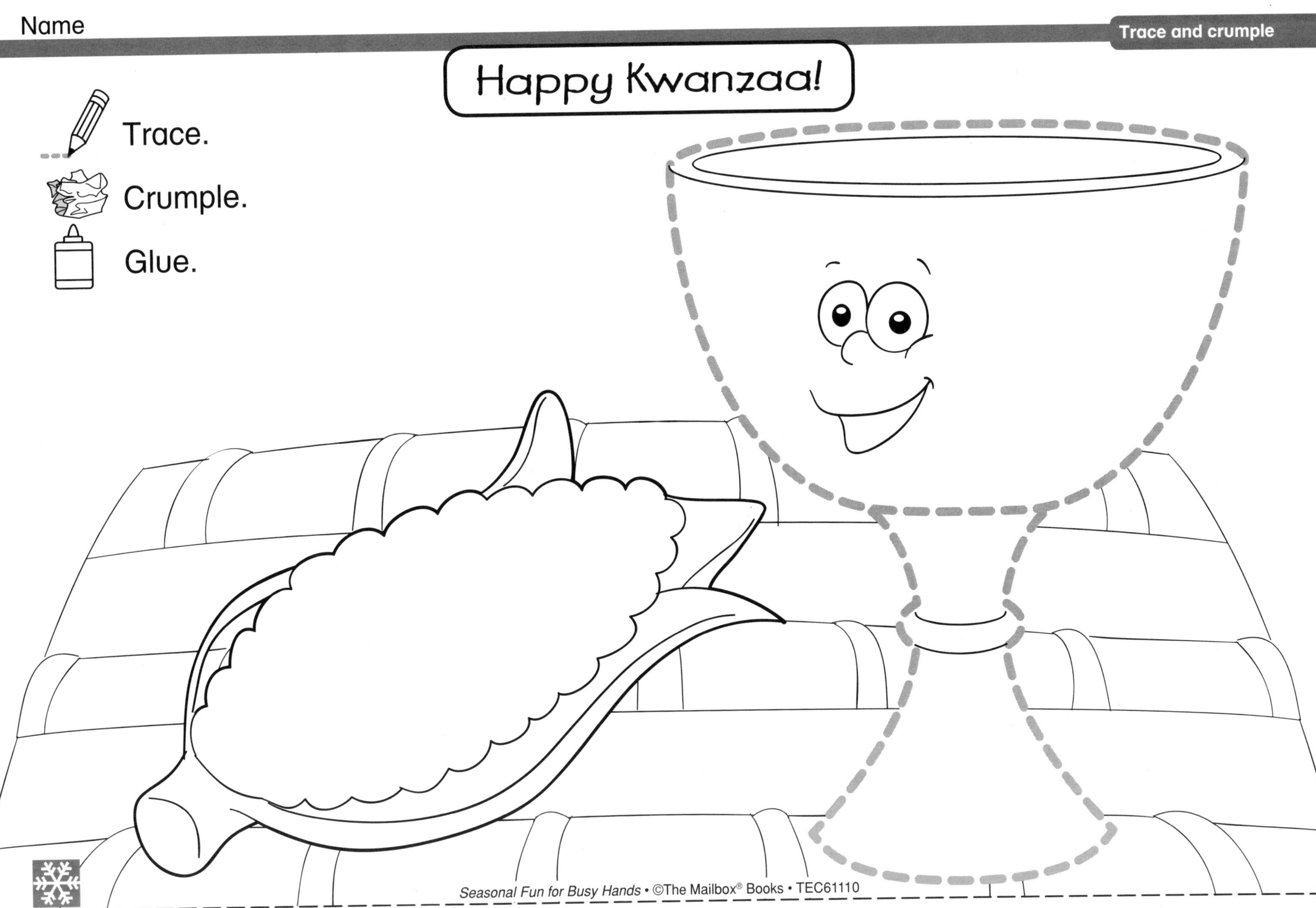

Note to the teacher: After the child finishes tracing, have him crumple yellow tissue paper squares and glue them to the corn so they resemble kernels.

Name

Winter Nap

Crumple.

Glue.

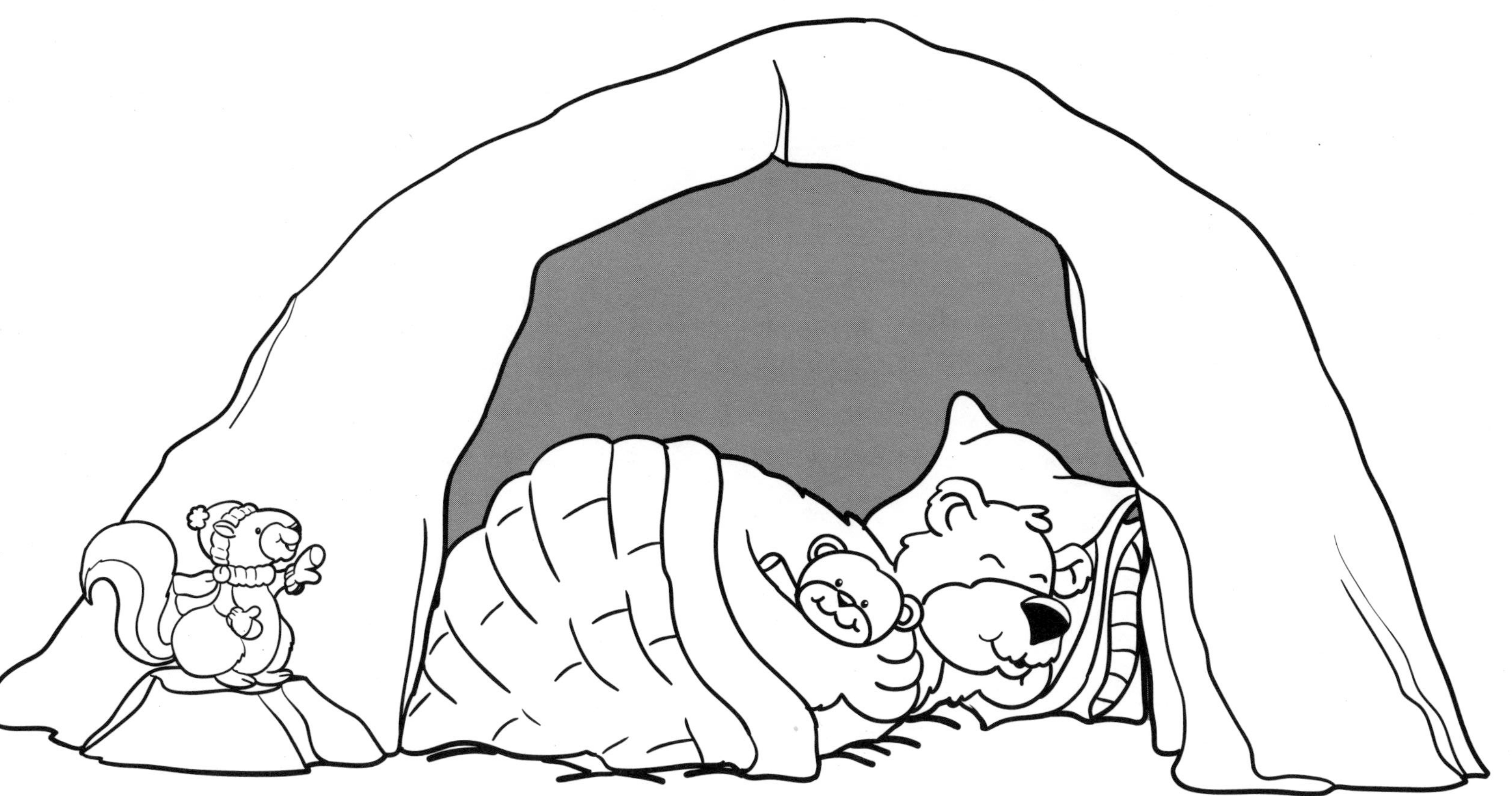

Note to the teacher: Copy the page on colored paper. Have students crumple squares of white tissue paper and glue them above and below the cave so they resemble snow.

Name

Snowpal's Friends

Trace.

Name

Sweet Treats

Tear.

Glue.

Note to the teacher: Have students tear white construction paper marshmallows and brown construction paper chocolate chips and glue them to the page as appropriate.

Name ________________

Penguins on Ice

Tear.

Glue.

Note to the teacher: Have students tear aluminum foil and glue it to the rink so it resembles ice.

Warm Winter Hat

Finish the hat.

Crumple.

Glue.

Note to the teacher: After drawing the hat, have students crumple tissue paper and glue it to the page to fill in the pom-pom and the cuff.

Name

Snug as a Bug

Cut.

Glue.

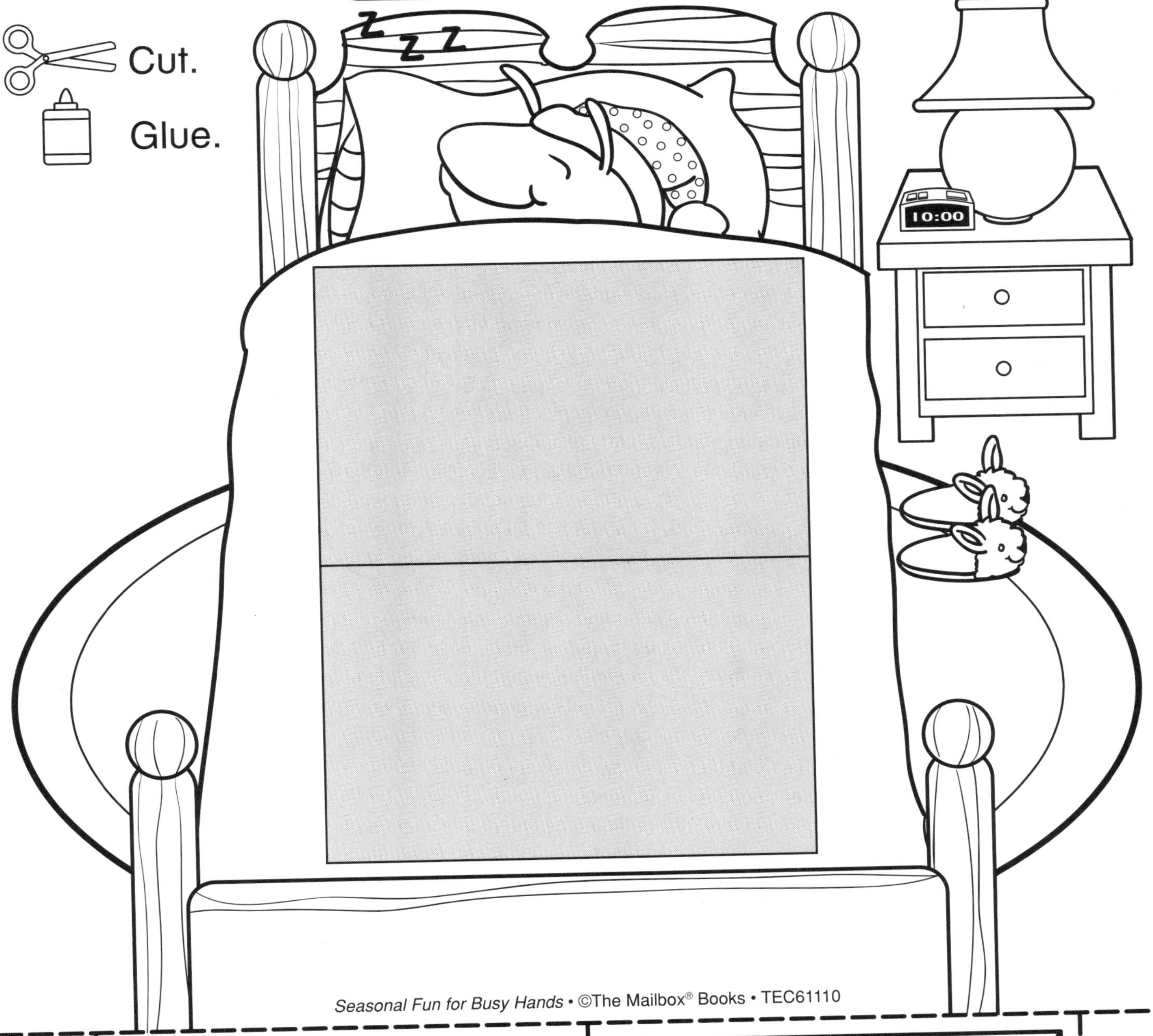

10:00

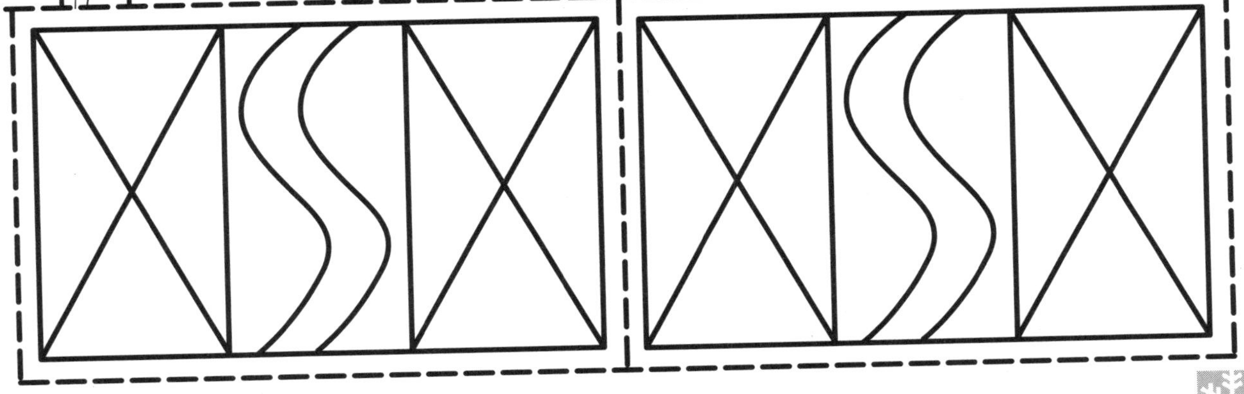

Name

Shiny Icicles

Tear.

Glue.

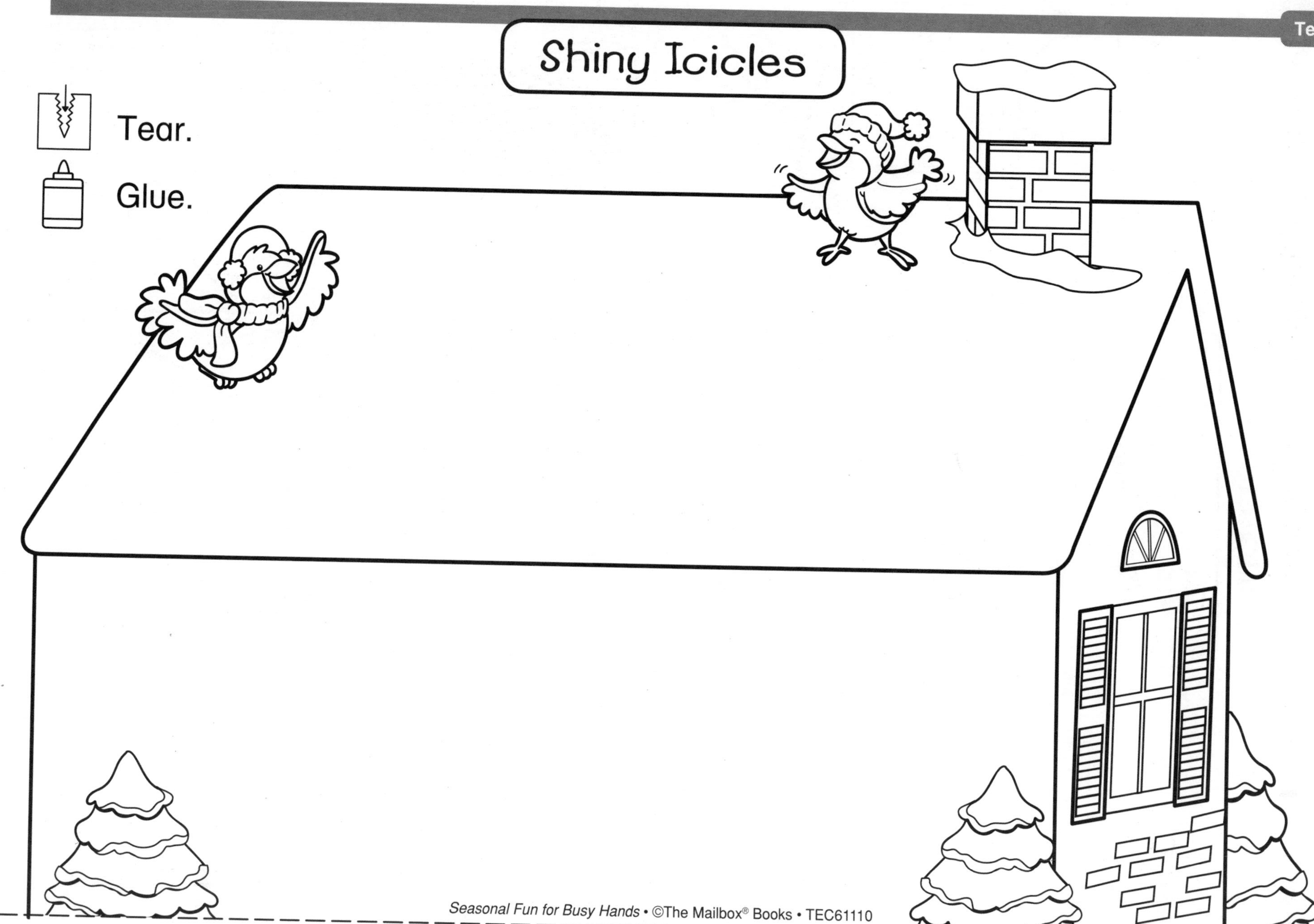

Note to the teacher: Give each student a three-inch-wide strip of aluminum foil. Have each child tear the foil into strips that resemble icicles to glue to the eaves of the house.

Name

Penguin's Place

Cut.

Glue.

Name

See the Shadow

Tear.

Glue.

 Note to the teacher: Have students tear pieces of black construction paper and glue them to the groundhog's shadow.

Name

Cozy Nest

Crumple.

Glue.

z z z z

Note to the teacher: Have students glue crumpled paper and other collage materials around the squirrel so they resemble a nest.

Name

Airmail

Trace.

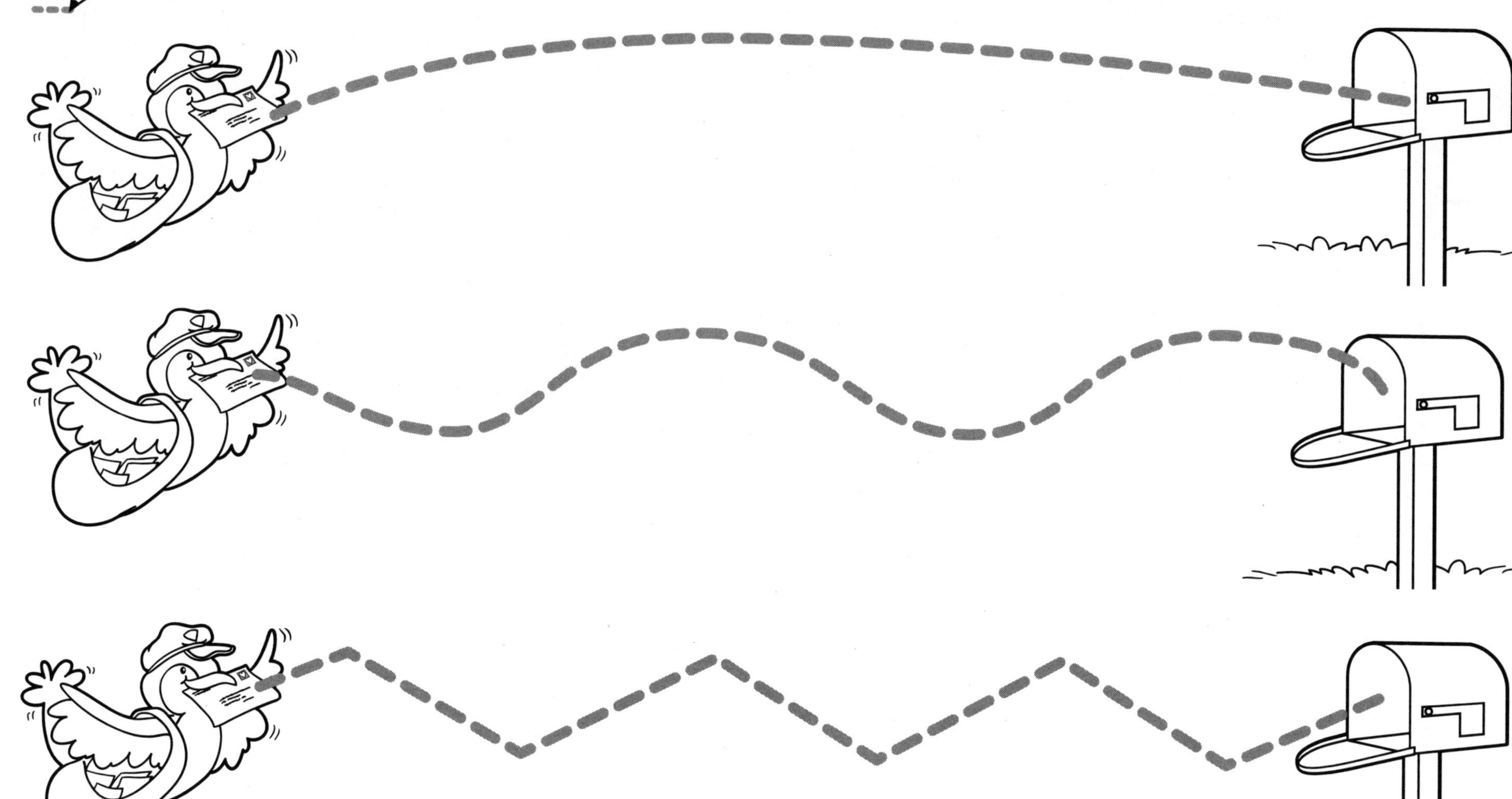

Name

Tasty Cake

Trace.

Name

Puppy Love

Draw ♡.

Name

Two Pieces Left!

Tear.

Cut.

Glue.

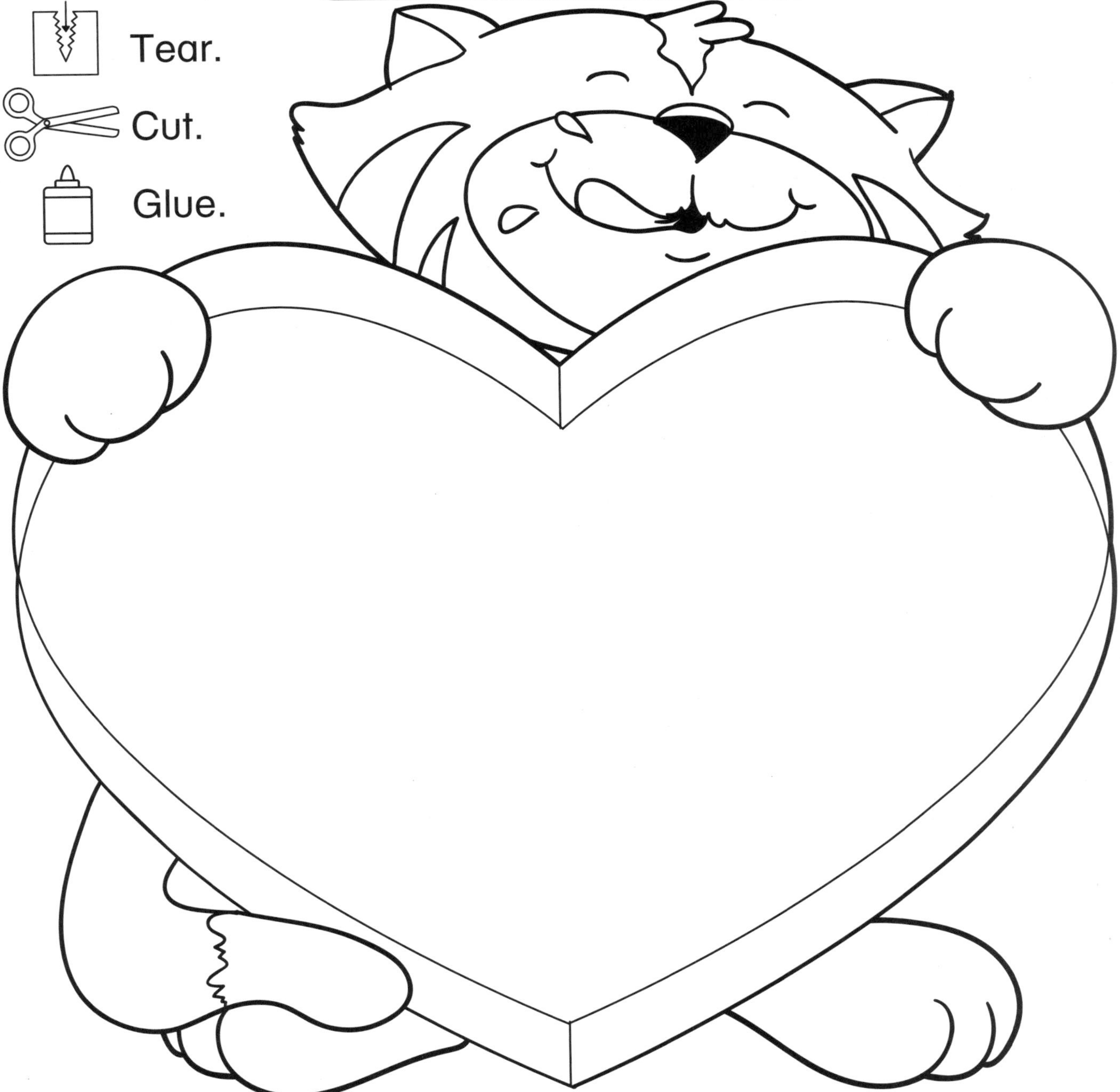

Note to the teacher: Have students tear pieces of red tissue paper and glue them inside the heart outline. Then have students cut out the pieces of candy and glue them to the heart.

Name

Pop the Balloons

Cut.

Name

Razzle-Dazzle Rainbow

Trace.

Name

1, 2, 3...Shamrock!

Cut.

Glue.

Name

Sweet Dreams

Trace.

$ $ $ $ $ $ $ $

Name

Lion and Lamb

 Draw ◯.

Name

In the Clouds

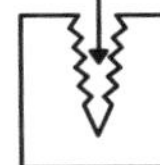 Tear.

 Glue.

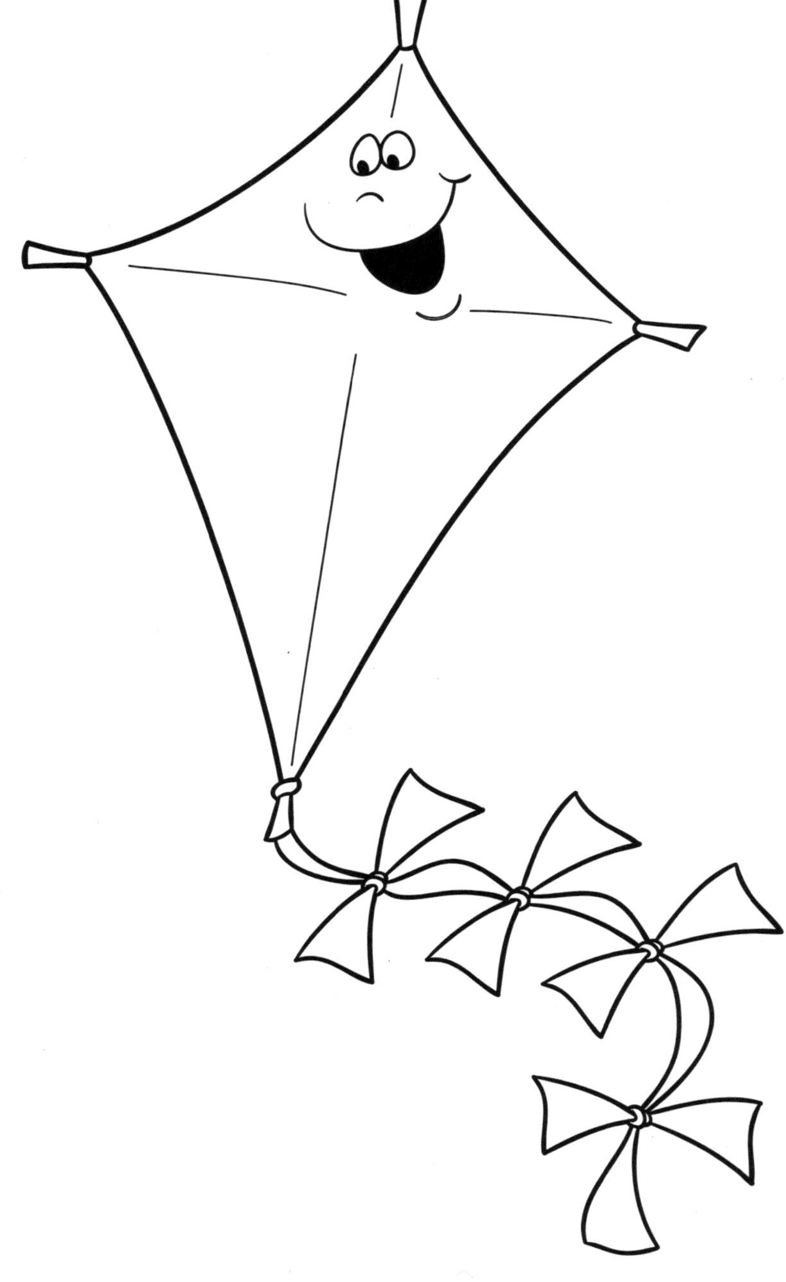

Note to the teacher: Copy this page on colored paper. Have students tear cotton balls and glue them around the kite so they resemble clouds.

Name

The Wind Blew...

 Trace.

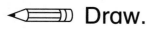

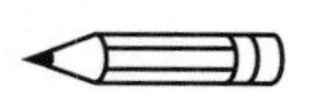 Draw.

Note to the teacher: Have students trace the lines and then draw an object that is being blown by the wind.

Name

Jelly Bean Bonanza!

Color.

Name

Supersize Lunch!

Tear.

Glue.

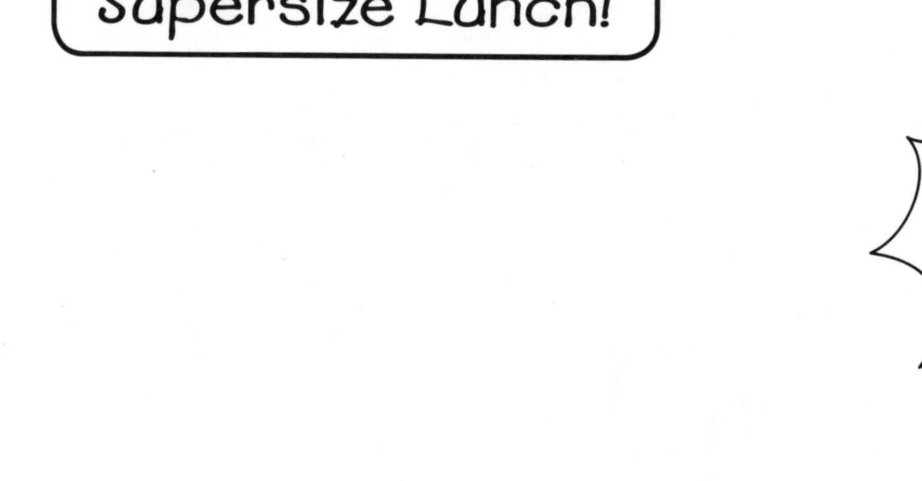

Note to the teacher: Have students tear green construction paper strips and glue them to the carrot tops so they resemble leaves.

Name

Bunny's Basket

Crumple.

Glue.

Note to the teacher: Have students crumple strips of green tissue paper so the paper resembles Easter grass and then glue the grass around the chocolate bunny.

Name

Spring Showers

 Tear.

 Glue.

 Note to the teacher: Have students tear blue construction paper scraps and glue them to the paper so they resemble raindrops.

Name

Trace.

Name

Awesome Blossoms

Crumple.

Glue.

Note to the teacher: Have students crumple squares of tissue paper and glue them to the center of each flower.

Name

Yummy Honey!

Draw / on the bee.

Name

Butterfly Shapes

Cut. Glue.

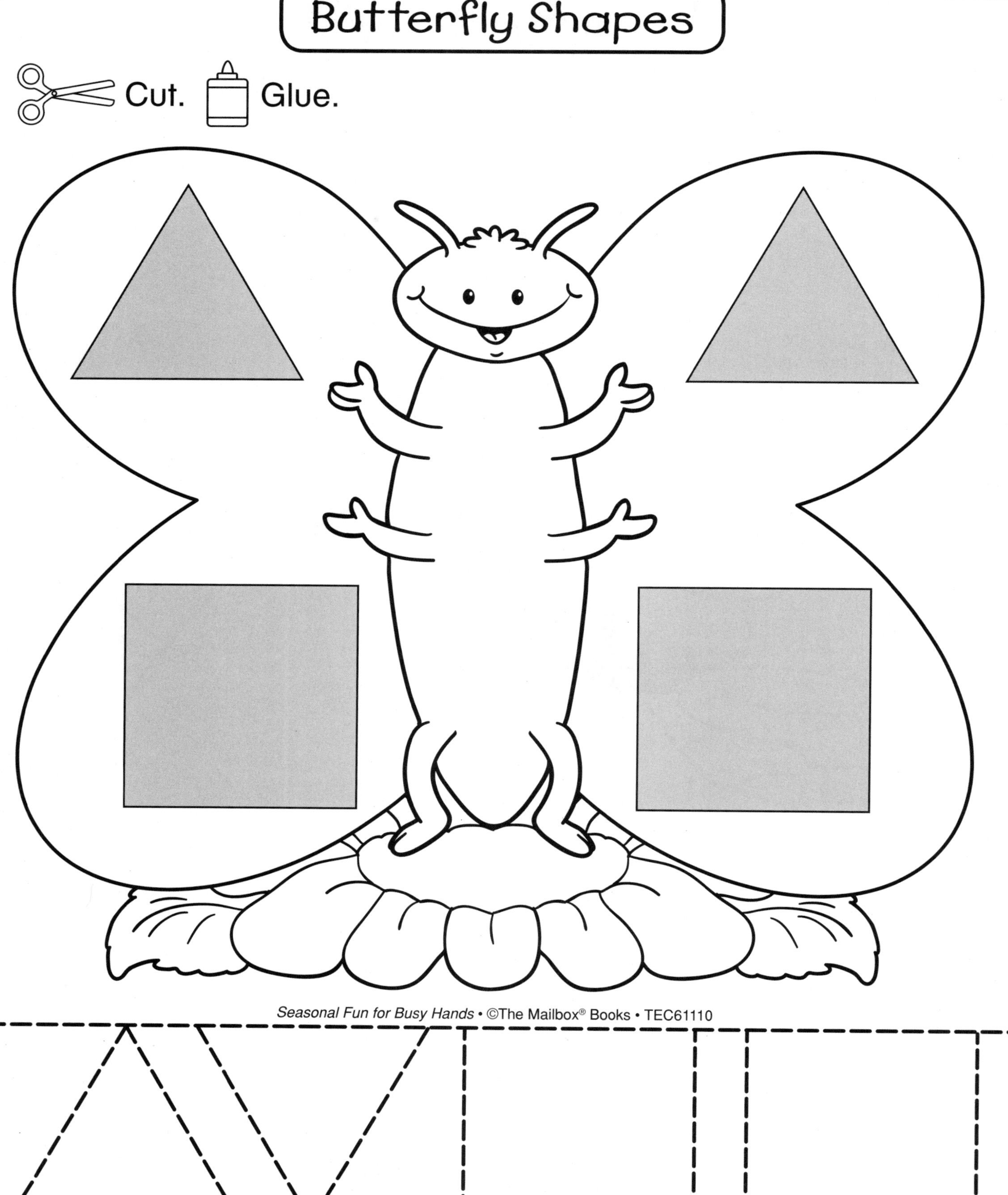

Name

Lazy Day

Trace.

Name

Slow Strolling

Tear.

Glue.

Note to the teacher: Have students tear different shades of green construction paper scraps and glue them to the turtle's shell.

Name

Cattail Cutouts

Cut.

Glue.

Name

Paddle, Baby Duck!

Color.

Name

Peep, Peep, Peep!

Cut.

Glue.

Name

Playful Piglets

Draw a tail on each piglet.

Color each pig.

Name

Ladybugs on the Move!

Trace.

Name

The Best Nest

Tear.

Glue.

Note to the teacher: Have students tear brown construction paper strips and glue them to the nest.

Name

Marvelous Mud!

Tear.

Glue.

Note to the teacher: Have students tear brown construction paper and glue it to the ground so it resembles mud.

Name

Fun at the Park

Trace.

Name

Lunch!

Trace.

Name

Busy Bees

Trace.

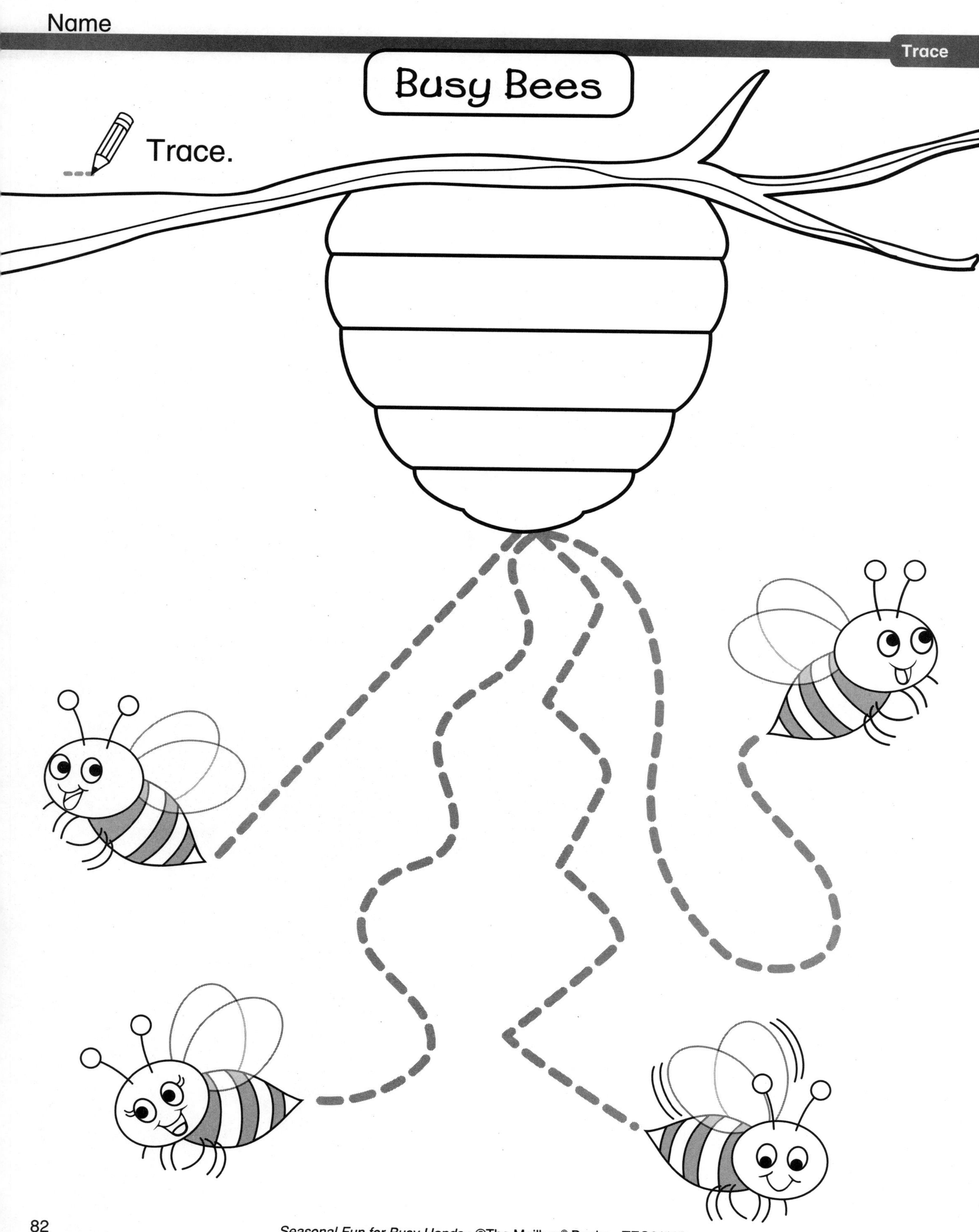

Name

Fun at the Beach

Trace.

Name

Bucket of Shells

Color.

Name

Ride the Waves!

Cut. Glue.

Tear. Glue.

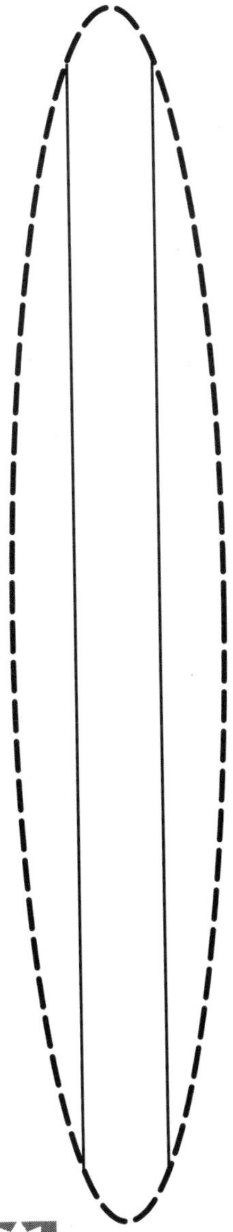

Note to the teacher: Have students glue the cutout to the page. Then have them tear blue tissue paper and glue it to the page so it resembles water.

Name

Cool Crab

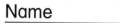

Tear.

Glue.

Note to the teacher: Have students tear strips of sandpaper and glue the strips to the page so they resemble sand.

Name

Back From the Beach

Cut.

Glue.

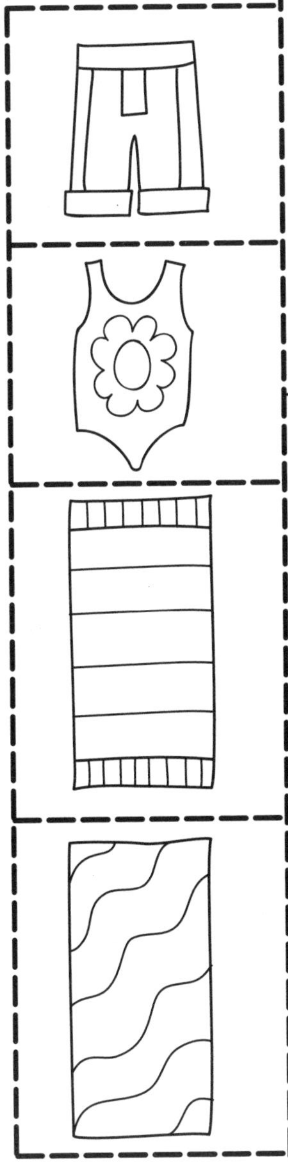

Name

Ice-Cold Lemonade

Cut.

Glue.

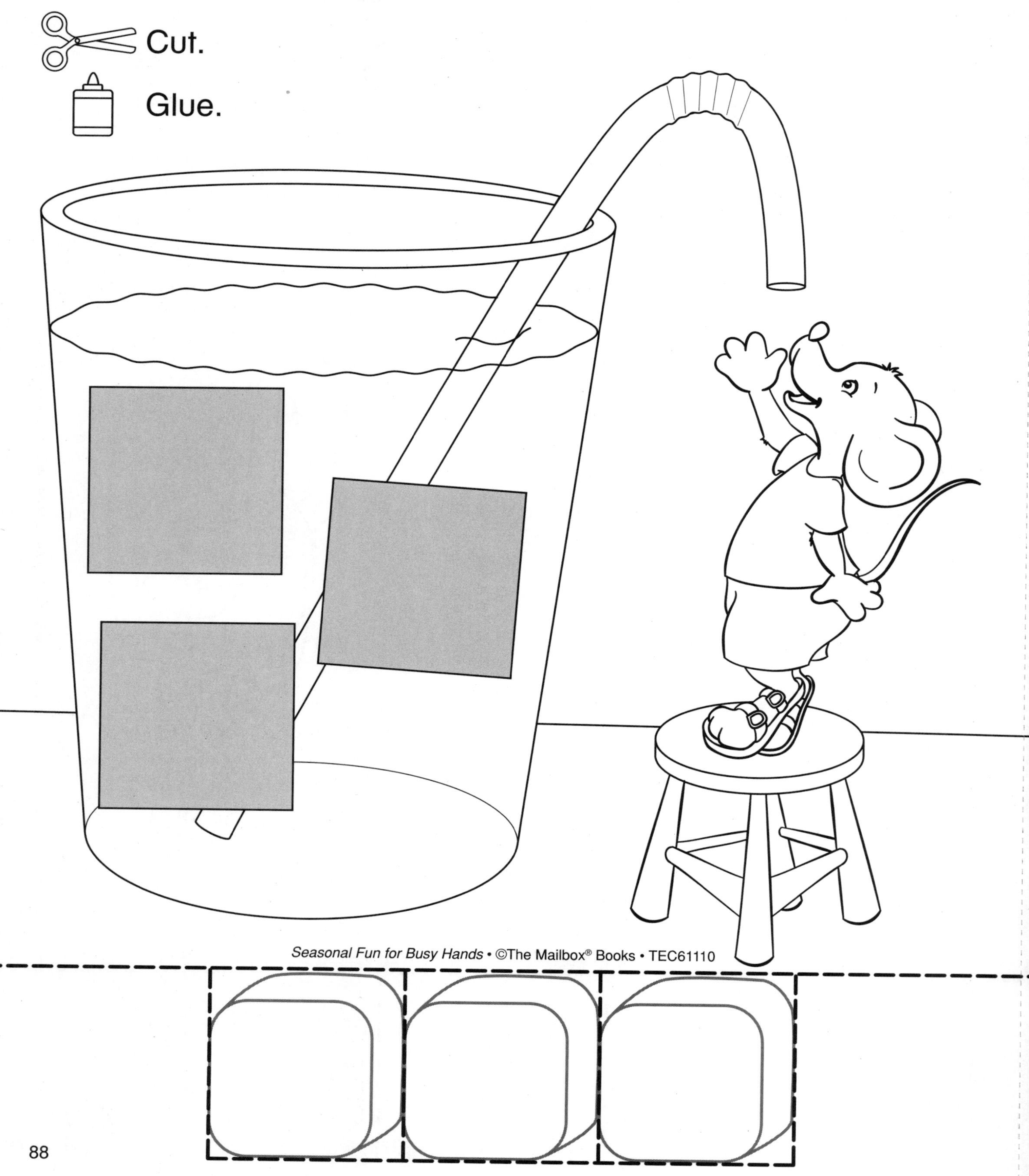

Name

A Treat for Two

Color.

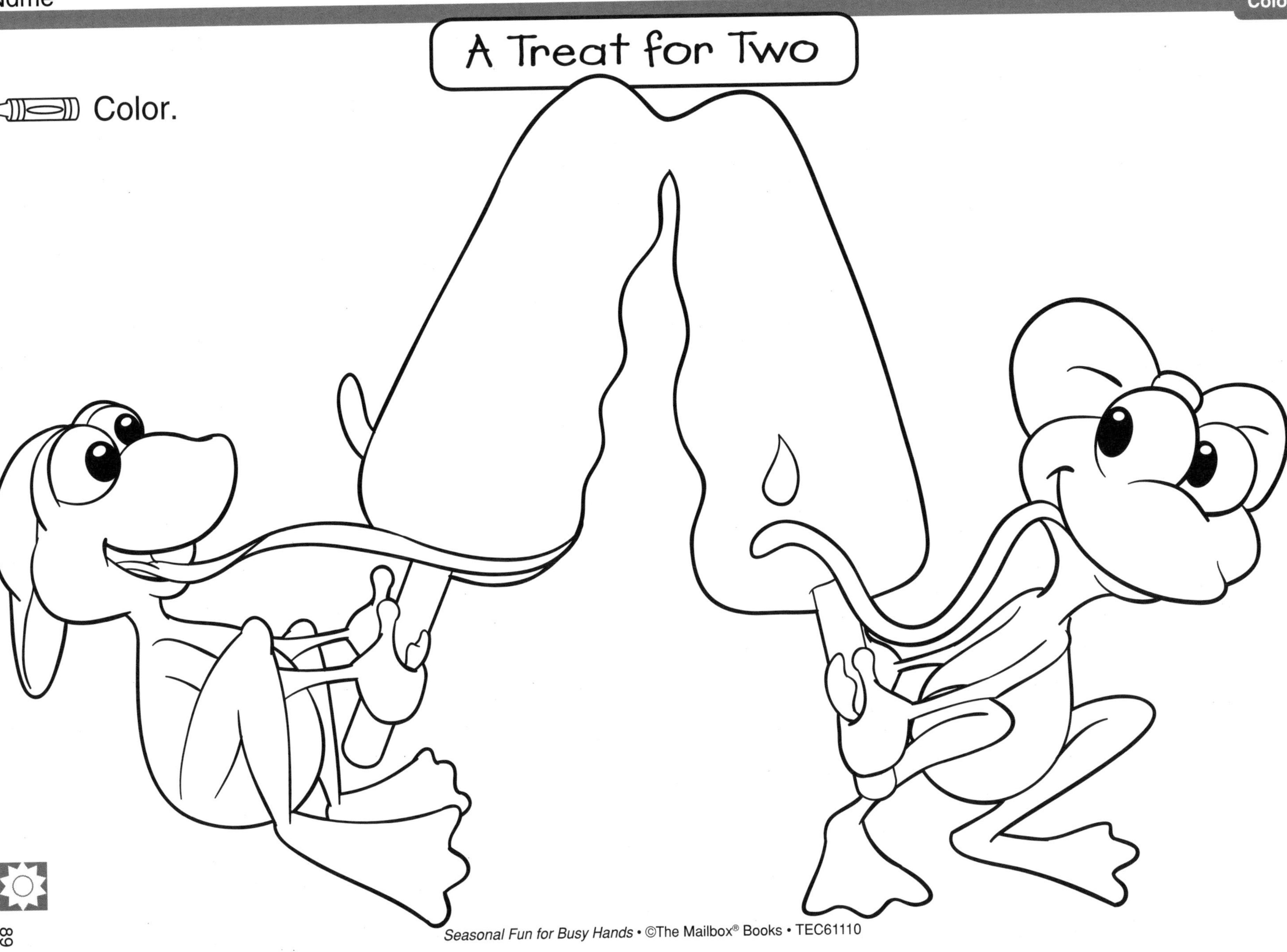

Name

Flamingos' Favorite Flavors

Name

Fantastic Fireworks!

Cut.

Name

Spectacular Sparklers!

Draw ✳ on each |.

Name

Tasty Tomatoes

Crumple.

Glue.

Note to the teacher: Have students crumple red tissue paper squares and glue them to the vines so they resemble tomatoes.

Name

Juicy Watermelon

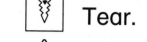

Tear.

Glue.

Note to the teacher: Have students tear black construction paper scraps and glue them to the watermelon so they resemble seeds.

Name

Gone Camping

Trace.

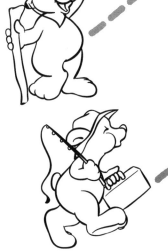

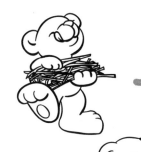

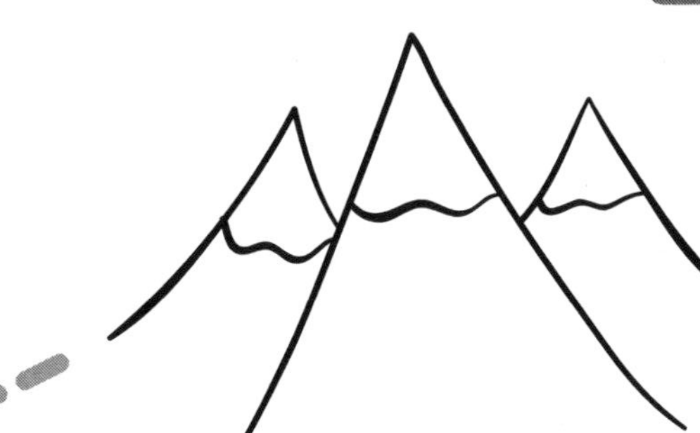
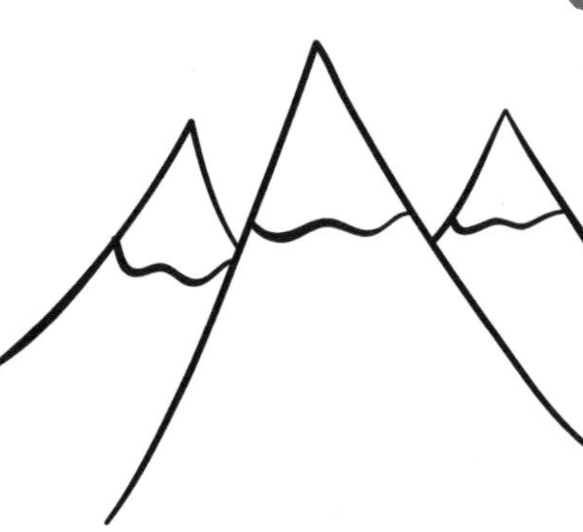

Name

Cut

Summer Sunshine

Cut.

Glue.

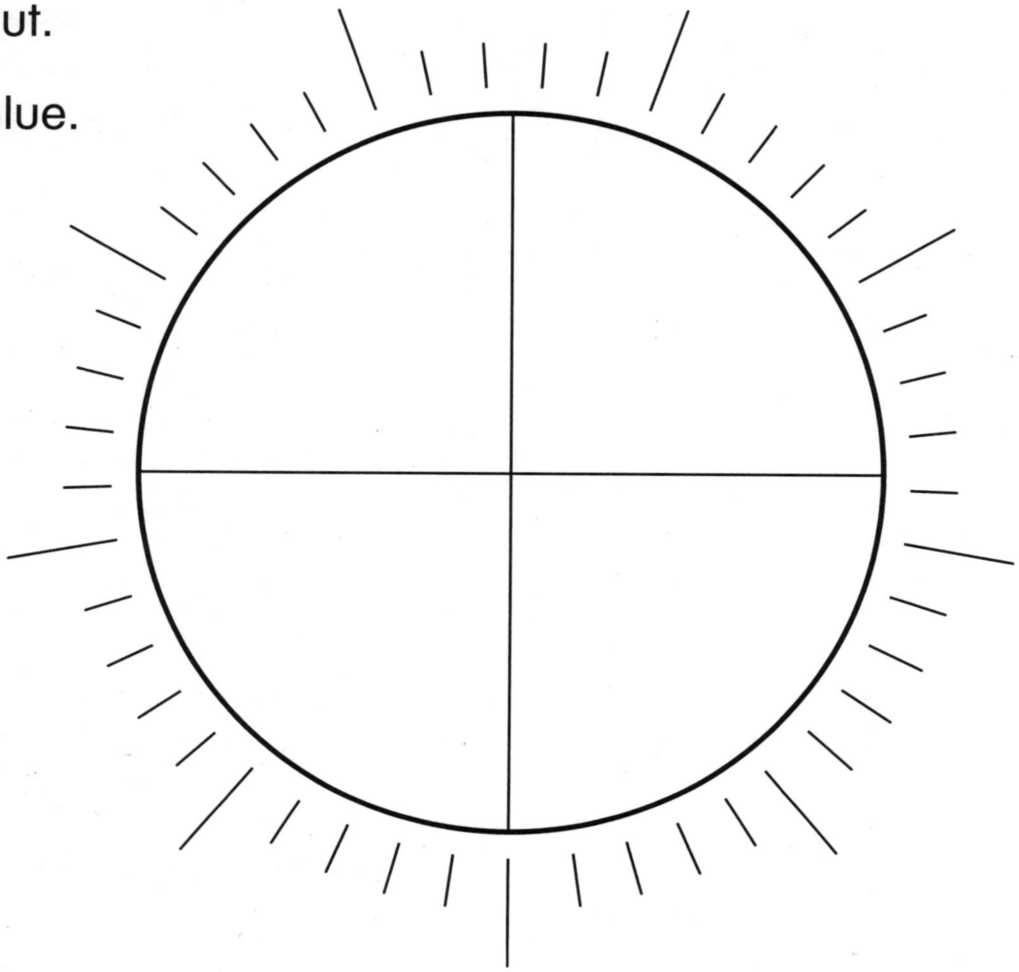

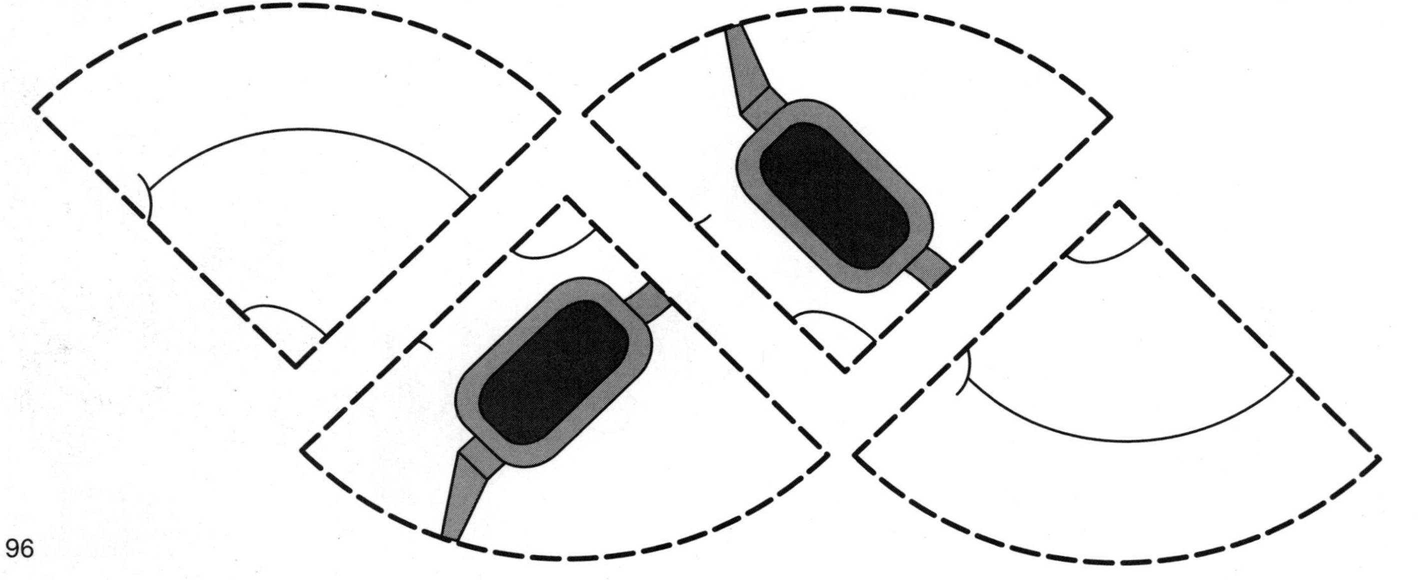